List
Your Self
for
Parents

❧

List Your Self *for* Parents

Listmaking as the Way to Celebrate and Enrich Parenting

Ilene Segalove, Paul Bob Velick, and Gareth Esersky

**Andrews McMeel
Publishing**

Kansas City

$\mathcal{T}$he LIST YOUR SELF book series
and calendars are the creation of
Ilene Segalove and Paul Bob Velick.
These listmaking tools invite the
reader to become the writer, offering an
interactive approach to self-discovery.

www.andrewsmcmeel.com

99 00 01 02 03 RDC 10 9 8 7 6 5 4 3 2 1

ISBN 0-8362-8180-2

Design by Holly Camerlinck

DEDICATION

To Dorinne and Stuart Velick, Elaine and Milton Segalove, and Rheta and Joseph Esersky—parents par excellence—to honor and celebrate their tenacity and faith, against all odds, that we'd ever grow up; and to the real kids, Charlotte, Amelia, and Zeke Blumenfeld.

CONTENTS

ACKNOWLEDGMENTS

The authors would like to express their heartfelt thanks to our terrific editor Chris Schillig and the Andrews McMeel sales force who made our first book, *List Your Self*, such a success; the readers of *List Your Self*; Jean Zevnik and our design team; Carol Mann, whose agency represents and encourages us; and, of course, the remarkable parents and children—including our own—whose lives, experience, and expertise inform these lists and enlighten the soul of this book.

INTRODUCTION

Sometimes it feels like becoming a parent happens overnight. One day you aren't a parent and the next day you're holding a child in your arms. Your life is changed forever. You have now assumed a role that affects every part of you, requires tremendous adjustments, and will bring rewards and joy you never could have imagined. As this miraculous new life comes into your home, so do the everyday trials of being a parent. It is a paradoxical situation, but one that gives you the chance to transform and grow in new and wonderful ways. While some folks will tell you there is no school to learn how to parent and "You just have to do the best you can," books by "experts" still come out every season with new "improved" ways to raise your kids right.

List Your Self for Parents is a different kind of parenting book. It gives you the opportunity to take a look at and appreciate your very personal style of parenting. Instead of spouting advice on the dos and don'ts of being the "perfect" parent, *List Your Self for Parents* is a chance to review, explore, and celebrate your own methods, beliefs, and accomplishments. This book asks you to think about yourself and your kids and what you've learned and discovered over the last few weeks, months, years, or decades. And it gives you the guidelines and the place to chronicle that valuable personal knowledge.

List Your Self for Parents is a way to develop a new relationship with your sometimes unexpressed self simply by asking you to fill in the blanks. Your answers to the 100 lists, organized in seven chapters, will let you articulate—from your heart and soul—what you think about being a parent.

With *List Your Self for Parents*, you will be able to recall
and record your best, most memorable, most outrageous, and
most touching experiences. You'll begin to notice the details of
daily life that make it all worthwhile. No matter the age of your
child, from infant to college student, it's never too early or too
late to begin listing. After the laundry is finished, the TV is
turned off, and the homework is done, *List Your Self for Parents*
is a place for you (and your partner) to go to and jot down a
quick list to reframe and reflect upon your day.

Putting pen to paper is a powerful act. And filling in a list
is a simple and easy way to deal with some of the ups and
downs of child rearing that might normally spin you out of con-
trol. For example, your kids just made a racket upstairs—sounds
like something dropped and spilled. You go mop up what looks
like an entire half-gallon of fruit juice, wash the floor, wash the
kids (again), change their pajamas, and put them to bed. You
are frazzled. You pick up *List Your Self for Parents* and fall into
chapter 3: "List your 'not-in-my-house' pronouncements." No
problem here. You've just dealt with answer number one:

- No food upstairs

You continue. Listing the rules of the house comes naturally.

- No skipping breakfast
- The "F" word
- Pierced body parts
- Deliberately hurting one another
- Any and all electronic toys

You are on a roll. This is fun. This is something you know
a lot about. Hey, you're an expert. And it feels good. Making a

list is a way of creating a little structure out of the chaos. Spilled fruit juice turns into a sequence of strong statements about your values, a litany of what's really important to you. From the ridiculous to the sublime in no time.

List Your Self for Parents is about you, the parent you are right now. It is not about how you should have handled the "terrible twos," or what was the "right" gift to buy your son for his birthday. And since you the reader becomes you the writer, over time the book will fill up with *your* answers and will become a treasured portrait of the "real" parent that you are . . . the who you are and what you feel and what you know about being a parent.

This is not a test! It's not a record that requires research and toil. Nor is it therapy, a self-help Band-Aid for problems or any kind of an instant fix. *List Your Self for Parents* is bigger than that; it's a collection of your reactions and feelings about the real nitty-gritty issues of child rearing and being a family. If you are fed up with your "picky eaters," make a list of all the foods you like to cook because your children eat them. Change your perspective for a moment. Jump into "List the meals you love to make because your kids love to eat them."

- Homemade macaroni and cheese
- Veal stew with sweet potatoes
- Lemon pudding
- Mystery sandwiches where something is hidden under melted cheese
- Anything with maple syrup

If you feel frustrated about not being prepared in one of a million situations, consider this: "List all the times you wished

you had a camera . . . and didn't." First you may feel plain guilty.
"Oh, I wish I had taken a picture of . . ." Start listing.

- Amelia in her first party dress
- The twins waltzing together, more or less
- Charlotte wearing that blue hat in a field of red tulips

As you list, your mood may shift a little. In the listing, those
moments will come alive for you once again. Listmaking is a
way of putting things on paper and putting them to rest. You
may have missed those colorful photographs, but the impact of
those memories lingers and they deserve to be written down.

Listmaking is a way of solidifying your insights and inspira-
tions by taking them out of your mind and putting them onto
the page. How about "List the most important qualities of
being a good parent" . . . or if you're brave, "List where you
come up short as a parent." You'll discover what really makes
you tick, and maybe even relive some of the most wonderful
moments of your life—just by scribbling your lists on these
pages. Or have a little fun and give yourself permission to remi-
nisce a little. "List what you miss most about life before kids."

- Coming home late
- Spontaneous sex
- Being in the bathroom alone for more than one minute
- Doing less laundry
- Going to the gym
- Wearing chic, expensive clothes that require dry cleaning
- Not having to answer a million questions

List Your Self for Parents can be used any time and any
place. Dive in, make a list, and change your tune. Chapter 1,

"Day-to-Day Life," is an easy place to list quickly and lift your mood. When you have more time, reflect on lists that are a little more philosophical. You may find chapter 4, "Values, Morality, and Discipline" and chapter 6, "Hopes and Dreams," good places to begin. Maybe you and your partner would like to list together. Find the list triggers that speak to both of you by randomly flipping through the pages. Choose one list, fill it out, and compare your answers. You may even find out some secrets about each other you never knew before. Or create a regular daily or weekly ritual of listing. Maybe on Sunday night, after things have settled, you'll cuddle up with *List Your Self for Parents* and complete the week by writing down your thoughts and feelings.

It's quite a journey from three A.M. feedings, through tantrums and tears, braces and dates, good grades and failures, and all the rest of the ups and downs of child rearing. Even on the worst day, when all you can think of is "I've had it!" and you wonder why you ever got into this game in the first place, you can vent it, let it all out, and "List all the things you resent about being a parent." Then, take a deep breath, relax, and "List all the things that you really like about being a parent."

- That costume I made was a good one
- I stay calm
- I treat my kids with respect
- I don't jump to conclusions . . . usually
- I am honest
- I try to listen
- I am fair
- My instincts are good and almost always correct
- I take true delight in my children

So pen your memories and insights, things to be thankful for, and all your worries. It needs to take only a minute or two, and you will find that the results are significant! Be brutally honest. Write as quickly or slowly as you like. Every day is different and every day is another list. You'll soothe your soul and renew yourself for the kid-filled days ahead. Years from now your children will thank you for filling in the blanks and creating a true-to-life portrait of their rich lives growing up. You'll be surprised to recognize the wealth of knowledge from your own hard-earned insights, understandings, successes, and failures.

These lists might hold your deepest feelings; embrace them and enjoy the time you spend listing. Here is where you get to reflect, rage, gloat, guffaw, proclaim, laugh, and love. The results are remarkable. Remember, parenting is simply one of the most important things you'll ever do, and while it may be the most difficult, it is also probably the most rewarding. Dive into *List Your Self for Parents* and renew and restore your appreciation for this awesome job you're doing. Listmaking will give you a new perspective from which to view your world, one that allows you to comprehend what you've given and what you've received. It is said that our need to love is greater than our need to be loved. Being a parent gives us the opportunity to love nonstop. Maybe in loving our children we can even learn to love ourselves a little bit more.

Ready, set, *list*!

CHAPTER 1

Day-to-Day Life

List the most beneficial day-to-day advice you give your kids.

_____

_____

_____

_____

_____

_____

_____

_____

_____

_____

_____

_____

_____

_____

_____

_____

_____

_____

_____

_____

*L*ist some of the shattered myths you've
faced about the joys of parenting.

_____

_____

_____

_____

_____

_____

_____

_____

_____

_____

_____

_____

_____

_____

_____

_____

_____

_____

List all the chores you feel the kids should be involved with around the house.

_____

_____

_____

_____

_____

_____

_____

_____

_____

_____

_____

_____

_____

_____

_____

_____

_____

_____

_____

_____

List the ways you've comforted your kids after a bad nightmare.

_____

_____

_____

_____

_____

_____

_____

_____

_____

_____

_____

_____

_____

_____

_____

_____

_____

_____

List the ways having kids has changed your relationship with your mate, for better or worse.

_____

_____

_____

_____

_____

_____

_____

_____

_____

_____

_____

_____

_____

_____

_____

_____

_____

_____

_____

_____

List what you miss most about your life before kids.

_____

_____

_____

_____

_____

_____

_____

_____

_____

_____

_____

_____

_____

_____

_____

_____

_____

_____

_____

_____

_____

_____

List the most common kid-related issues your mate and you disagree about.

List all the ways you've made your home "kidproof."

_____

_____

_____

_____

_____

_____

_____

_____

_____

_____

_____

_____

_____

_____

_____

_____

_____

_____

_____

_____

_____

List all the places you must attend as a parent you wouldn't ordinarily choose to go.

_____

_____

_____

_____

_____

_____

_____

_____

_____

_____

_____

_____

_____

_____

_____

_____

_____

_____

_____

_____

_____

List the names you've called your child, both good and bad.

_____

_____

_____

_____

_____

_____

_____

_____

_____

_____

_____

_____

_____

_____

_____

_____

_____

_____

_____

_____

List the qualities you require in your kids' caregiver/nanny.

_____

_____

_____

_____

_____

_____

_____

_____

_____

_____

_____

_____

_____

_____

_____

_____

_____

_____

_____

_____

List the phrases you keep repeating, like "Brush your teeth; do your homework; where are you going?"

*L*ist the meals you love to make because your kids love to eat them.

List how you can get involved with your kids' school.

❧

CHAPTER 2

Memorable Moments

List the most memorable conversations you've had with your kids and what they were about.

_____

_____

_____

_____

_____

_____

_____

_____

_____

_____

_____

_____

_____

_____

_____

_____

_____

_____

List the gifts you've received from your kids that you'll always treasure.

_____

_____

_____

_____

_____

_____

_____

_____

_____

_____

_____

_____

_____

_____

_____

_____

_____

_____

_____

_____

_____

List the funny or personally embarrassing things you have willingly done for your kids.

_____

_____

_____

_____

_____

_____

_____

_____

_____

_____

_____

_____

_____

_____

_____

_____

_____

_____

_____

_____

_____

List all the things you do as a family that you'll never forget.

---

*List the most loving things your kids
have said to you.*

_____

_____

_____

_____

_____

_____

_____

_____

_____

_____

_____

_____

_____

_____

_____

_____

_____

_____

List the truly wacky, funny things your kids have done.

_____

_____

_____

_____

_____

_____

_____

_____

_____

_____

_____

_____

_____

_____

_____

_____

_____

_____

_____

List the many joys and fears you felt when your child was born.

_____

_____

_____

_____

_____

_____

_____

_____

_____

_____

_____

_____

_____

_____

_____

_____

_____

_____

List your kids' clothes/toys/stuff you can't bear to give away, even though your kids have outgrown them.

_____

_____

_____

_____

_____

_____

_____

_____

_____

_____

_____

_____

_____

_____

_____

_____

_____

_____

_____

_____

List your child's first phrases.

_____

_____

_____

_____

_____

_____

_____

_____

_____

_____

_____

_____

_____

_____

_____

_____

_____

_____

_____

_____

_____

List all the little things your kids do that just make your heart melt.

_____

_____

_____

_____

_____

_____

_____

_____

_____

_____

_____

_____

_____

_____

_____

_____

_____

_____

_____

_____

_____

_____

List the things about yourself that you want your children to remember always.

_____

_____

_____

_____

_____

_____

_____

_____

_____

_____

_____

_____

_____

_____

_____

_____

_____

_____

_____

_____

_____

List the way you felt when you dropped your kids off the first day of school.

_____

_____

_____

_____

_____

_____

_____

_____

_____

_____

_____

_____

_____

_____

_____

_____

_____

List the special holidays and birthdays
your kids will always remember.

_____

_____

_____

_____

_____

_____

_____

_____

_____

_____

_____

_____

_____

_____

_____

_____

_____

_____

List some of the best things your kids have told you about yourself.

List what your kids do that makes you feel your proudest.

List the momentos and treasures you'll want to pass on to your kids.

_____

_____

_____

_____

_____

_____

_____

_____

_____

_____

_____

_____

_____

_____

_____

_____

_____

_____

_____

_____

List all the reasons you are grateful you have kids.

_____

_____

_____

_____

_____

_____

_____

_____

_____

_____

_____

_____

_____

_____

_____

_____

_____

_____

_____

_____

CHAPTER 3

How Am I Doing?

*L*ist all the things that you really like about yourself as a parent.

_____

_____

_____

_____

_____

_____

_____

_____

_____

_____

_____

_____

_____

_____

_____

_____

_____

_____

_____

List the most hurtful things your kids have said to you.

_____

_____

_____

_____

_____

_____

_____

_____

_____

_____

_____

_____

_____

_____

_____

_____

_____

_____

_____

_____

List your biggest parental worries—the rational and irrational ones—that keep you up at night.

_____

_____

_____

_____

_____

_____

_____

_____

_____

_____

_____

_____

_____

_____

_____

_____

_____

_____

List the ways you keep your sense of humor about being a mom or dad.

_____

_____

_____

_____

_____

_____

_____

_____

_____

_____

_____

_____

_____

_____

_____

_____

_____

_____

_____

List the ways you have encouraged and helped your kids identify and reach new goals.

_____

_____

_____

_____

_____

_____

_____

_____

_____

_____

_____

_____

_____

_____

_____

_____

_____

_____

_____

List the most demanding, frustrating,
or challenging aspects of parenting.

_____

_____

_____

_____

_____

_____

_____

_____

_____

_____

_____

_____

_____

_____

_____

_____

_____

_____

_____

List what your child does or says that makes you know you've done a good job parenting.

*L*ist the most rewarding, joyous, top-of-the-pop aspects of parenting.

_____

_____

_____

_____

_____

_____

_____

_____

_____

_____

_____

_____

_____

_____

_____

_____

_____

_____

_____

*L*ist the words of wisdom you want to
make sure you pass on to your kids.

_____

_____

_____

_____

_____

_____

_____

_____

_____

_____

_____

_____

_____

_____

_____

_____

_____

_____

_____

_____

*L*ist *where you come up short as a parent.*

_____

_____

_____

_____

_____

_____

_____

_____

_____

_____

_____

_____

_____

_____

_____

_____

_____

_____

_____

_____

_____

List the most important qualities of being a good parent.

_____

_____

_____

_____

_____

_____

_____

_____

_____

_____

_____

_____

_____

_____

_____

_____

_____

_____

_____

_____

List the advice that comes out of your mouth that you thought you'd never say.

_____

_____

_____

_____

_____

_____

_____

_____

_____

_____

_____

_____

_____

_____

_____

_____

_____

_____

_____

_____

_____

_____

List all the characteristics you just adore
in your kids.

List what you do when you are spending "quality" time with your kids.

_____
_____
_____
_____
_____
_____
_____
_____
_____
_____
_____
_____
_____
_____
_____
_____
_____
_____
_____
_____
_____

List the ways your partner shows himself or herself to be a great parent.

_____

_____

_____

_____

_____

_____

_____

_____

_____

_____

_____

_____

_____

_____

_____

_____

_____

_____

_____

_____

List what being a parent has taught you about yourself.

_____

_____

_____

_____

_____

_____

_____

_____

_____

_____

_____

_____

_____

_____

_____

_____

_____

_____

List your "not-in-my-house" pronouncements.

~

CHAPTER 4

Values, Morality, and Discipline

List some of the "everybody's doing it" stuff you hate.

_____

_____

_____

_____

_____

_____

_____

_____

_____

_____

_____

_____

_____

_____

_____

_____

_____

_____

_____

List the things you want your kids to avoid.

_____

_____

_____

_____

_____

_____

_____

_____

_____

_____

_____

_____

_____

_____

_____

_____

List the most provocative questions your kid has ever asked you about God.

_____

_____

_____

_____

_____

_____

_____

_____

_____

_____

_____

_____

_____

_____

_____

_____

_____

_____

_____

_____

*L*ist the ways you've catered to your kids' demands when you wished you hadn't.

_____

_____

_____

_____

_____

_____

_____

_____

_____

_____

_____

_____

_____

_____

_____

_____

_____

_____

_____

List the most difficult questions your kids have ever asked you about sex.

_____

_____

_____

_____

_____

_____

_____

_____

_____

_____

_____

_____

_____

_____

_____

_____

_____

_____

_____

_____

*L*ist all the ways you try to protect your
kids from growing up too fast.

_____

_____

_____

_____

_____

_____

_____

_____

_____

_____

_____

_____

_____

_____

_____

_____

_____

_____

_____

_____

_____

List the key life events that have shaped your child's character.

_____

_____

_____

_____

_____

_____

_____

_____

_____

_____

_____

_____

_____

_____

_____

_____

_____

_____

_____

_____

List your many definitions of family: "A family is . . ."

_____

_____

_____

_____

_____

_____

_____

_____

_____

_____

_____

_____

_____

_____

_____

_____

_____

_____

_____

_____

List the basic human values your children need to grow up knowing.

_____

_____

_____

_____

_____

_____

_____

_____

_____

_____

_____

_____

_____

_____

_____

_____

_____

_____

_____

_____

_____

List the ways you instill confidence in your children.

_____

_____

_____

_____

_____

_____

_____

_____

_____

_____

_____

_____

_____

_____

_____

_____

_____

_____

_____

_____

List all the fair punishments you dish out if your kids misbehave.

_____

_____

_____

_____

_____

_____

_____

_____

_____

_____

_____

_____

_____

_____

_____

_____

_____

_____

_____

*L*ist all the behaviors that are totally
unacceptable in your kids.

_____

_____

_____

_____

_____

_____

_____

_____

_____

_____

_____

_____

_____

_____

_____

_____

_____

_____

_____

_____

_____

List all the scary things you've said to make your kids behave properly.

CHAPTER 5

When I Was Your Age

*L*ist the stuff you did as a kid that you want your kids to do.

List what you've taught your children about life that you wish you'd known when you were a kid.

_____

_____

_____

_____

_____

_____

_____

_____

_____

_____

_____

_____

_____

_____

_____

_____

_____

_____

_____

_____

*L*ist some of your kids' "off-the-wall"
traits that make them "your" kids.

_____

_____

_____

_____

_____

_____

_____

_____

_____

_____

_____

_____

_____

_____

_____

_____

_____

_____

_____

_____

List what you are most grateful for about the way your kids have turned out.

_____
_____
_____
_____
_____
_____
_____
_____
_____
_____
_____
_____
_____
_____
_____
_____
_____
_____
_____
_____

List all the ways you want to raise your kids differently from the way you were brought up.

_____

_____

_____

_____

_____

_____

_____

_____

_____

_____

_____

_____

_____

_____

_____

_____

_____

_____

_____

_____

_____

List the books, movies, and other delights
from your own childhood that you must
share with your children.

_____

_____

_____

_____

_____

_____

_____

_____

_____

_____

_____

_____

_____

_____

_____

_____

_____

_____

*L*ist how your school days were different from your kids'.

_____

_____

_____

_____

_____

_____

_____

_____

_____

_____

_____

_____

_____

_____

_____

_____

_____

_____

_____

List how you are acting like your own
parents, good and bad.

_____

_____

_____

_____

_____

_____

_____

_____

_____

_____

_____

_____

_____

_____

_____

_____

_____

_____

_____

List how your parents treat you differently now that you are a parent.

_____

_____

_____

_____

_____

_____

_____

_____

_____

_____

_____

_____

_____

_____

_____

_____

_____

_____

List all the dangerous weird stuff you did as a child that you hope your children won't do.

_____

_____

_____

_____

_____

_____

_____

_____

_____

_____

_____

_____

_____

_____

_____

_____

_____

_____

_____

_____

List all the things you say to your kids that your parents said to you and you can't believe you are saying but you are.

_____
_____
_____
_____
_____
_____
_____
_____
_____
_____
_____
_____
_____
_____
_____
_____
_____
_____
_____

*L*ist all the great parents you remember
from your childhood (TV parents are
okay).

_____

_____

_____

_____

_____

_____

_____

_____

_____

_____

_____

_____

_____

_____

_____

_____

_____

_____

_____

_____

_____

List the ways being a parent has helped you to understand your parents a lot better.

_____

_____

_____

_____

_____

_____

_____

_____

_____

_____

_____

_____

_____

_____

_____

_____

_____

_____

_____

List how you feel when you realize your kids are a lot like you.

_____

_____

_____

_____

_____

_____

_____

_____

_____

_____

_____

_____

_____

_____

_____

_____

_____

_____

_____

_____

❧

CHAPTER 6

Hopes and Dreams

List what you've learned from your kids.

List the dreams or fantasies you have for your kids' future.

_____

_____

_____

_____

_____

_____

_____

_____

_____

_____

_____

_____

_____

_____

_____

_____

_____

_____

_____

_____

List the qualities you hope your kids inherited from you and your mate.

_____

_____

_____

_____

_____

_____

_____

_____

_____

_____

_____

_____

_____

_____

_____

_____

_____

_____

_____

List the skills you want to encourage in your kids.

_____

_____

_____

_____

_____

_____

_____

_____

_____

_____

_____

_____

_____

_____

_____

_____

_____

_____

_____

List how you feel when you see your kids perform on stage, play sports, or excel in anything.

_____

_____

_____

_____

_____

_____

_____

_____

_____

_____

_____

_____

_____

_____

_____

_____

_____

_____

_____

List the fantasies you have for your children's lives that you had better keep to yourself.

_____

_____

_____

_____

_____

_____

_____

_____

_____

_____

_____

_____

_____

_____

_____

_____

_____

_____

_____

_____

*L*ist the hobbies, sports, or musical interests you want to support in your kids' lives.

_____

_____

_____

_____

_____

_____

_____

_____

_____

_____

_____

_____

_____

_____

_____

_____

_____

_____

_____

_____

_____

List all the honors, big deals, and accomplishments you "just know" your kids will garner.

_____

_____

_____

_____

_____

_____

_____

_____

_____

_____

_____

_____

_____

_____

_____

_____

_____

_____

_____

List the elements of a perfect environment in which to raise children.

_____

_____

_____

_____

_____

_____

_____

_____

_____

_____

_____

_____

_____

_____

_____

_____

_____

_____

_____

_____

_____

_____

_____

List the qualities of a perfect child.

_____

_____

_____

_____

_____

_____

_____

_____

_____

_____

_____

_____

_____

_____

_____

_____

_____

_____

List the celebrations and events you hope to share with your kids.

_____

_____

_____

_____

_____

_____

_____

_____

_____

_____

_____

_____

_____

_____

_____

_____

_____

_____

_____

What if you could introduce your kids to anyone in history? List all the people you'd want them to meet.

_____

_____

_____

_____

_____

_____

_____

_____

_____

_____

_____

_____

_____

_____

_____

_____

_____

_____

❧

CHAPTER 7

Single Parents

List the strategies and positive thinking that have helped you through the most difficult parts of parenting so far.

_____

_____

_____

_____

_____

_____

_____

_____

_____

_____

_____

_____

_____

_____

_____

_____

_____

List what you love about being a single parent.

_____

_____

_____

_____

_____

_____

_____

_____

_____

_____

_____

_____

_____

_____

_____

_____

_____

_____

_____

_____

List what you hate about being a single parent.

_____

_____

_____

_____

_____

_____

_____

_____

_____

_____

_____

_____

_____

_____

_____

_____

_____

_____

List how the world treats you differently because you are a single parent.

_____

_____

_____

_____

_____

_____

_____

_____

_____

_____

_____

_____

_____

_____

_____

_____

_____

_____

_____

_____

List your kids' complaints about being raised by a single parent.

_____

_____

_____

_____

_____

_____

_____

_____

_____

_____

_____

_____

_____

_____

_____

_____

_____

_____

List what you think your kids may miss, being brought up with only one worldview and experience—yours.

_____

_____

_____

_____

_____

_____

_____

_____

_____

_____

_____

_____

_____

_____

_____

_____

_____

_____

List the support you receive from friends and relatives that makes you feel grateful.

_____

_____

_____

_____

_____

_____

_____

_____

_____

_____

_____

_____

_____

_____

_____

_____

_____

_____

_____

_____

List the financial concerns you have because you are the only source of income.

_____

_____

_____

_____

_____

_____

_____

_____

_____

_____

_____

_____

_____

_____

_____

_____

_____

_____

_____

List how, in the best of all possible worlds, you would do things differently.

_____

_____

_____

_____

_____

_____

_____

_____

_____

_____

_____

_____

_____

_____

_____

_____

_____

_____

_____

List your concerns about being the only parent of a child of the opposite gender: moms/sons; dads/daughters.

_____

_____

_____

_____

_____

_____

_____

_____

_____

_____

_____

_____

_____

_____

_____

_____

*L*ist the terrific things your kids do to
help you.

_____

_____

_____

_____

_____

_____

_____

_____

_____

_____

_____

_____

_____

_____

_____

_____

_____

_____

_____

_____

_____

_____

_____

List how you have tried to do special things to make up for being a single parent.

_____

_____

_____

_____

_____

_____

_____

_____

_____

_____

_____

_____

_____

_____

_____

_____

_____

_____

_____

_____

List the satisfaction you receive from being a good single parent.

_____

_____

_____

_____

_____

_____

_____

_____

_____

_____

_____

_____

_____

_____

_____

_____

_____

_____

_____

_____